MW00353755

49 Trout Streams of New Mexico

49 Trout Streams
of New Mexico

Raymond C. Shewnack

William J. Frangos

UNIVERSITY OF NEW MEXICO PRESS
ALBUQUERQUE

© 2006 by the University of New Mexico Press
All rights reserved. Published 2006
Printed and bound in China through Four Colour Imports, Ltd.

YEAR   PRINTING
12 11 10 09 08   3 4 5 6 7

Library of Congress Cataloging-in-Publication Data

Shewnack, Raymond C., 1949–
  49 trout streams of New Mexico / Raymond C. Shewnack, William J. Frangos.
      p. cm.
  ISBN-13: 978-0-8263-3718-4 (pbk. : alk. paper)
  ISBN-10: 0-8263-3718-X (pbk. : alk. paper)
  1. Trout fishing—New Mexico. 2. Rivers—New Mexico.
  I. Title: Forty-nine trout streams of New Mexico. II. Frangos, William. III. Title.
  SH688.U6S54 2006
  799.17'5709789—dc22
                              2006005508

Photographs by Bill Frangos and Ray Shewnack
Maps by Juaquin Sanchez

Book design and composition by Damien Shay
Body type is Minion 10/14
Display is ExPonto and Raleigh

Table of Contents

Acknowledgments

WE ARE FORTUNATE to have family and friends who support our obsession.

First and foremost, we wish to thank our wives, Ann and Adele, for their love and understanding. They recognize our obsession with rivers. They have never allowed us to fish. Rather they encourage us to hone our angling skills and pursue our appreciation of the art.

We count on our cherished children, Katelyn, Ashley, Adam, and Vanessa, for their ability to love and encourage us in spite of our faults and mistakes.

We thank our many angling partners who teach us something new every time we are together. They have nurtured our passion for fly-fishing, but most importantly they are friends when we are not on a stream.

We owe our gratitude to two angling authors who paved the way to the rivers. Ti Piper's *Fishing in New Mexico* and Craig Martin's *Fly Fishing in Northern New Mexico* were constant companions in our travels. Their directions for access proved valuable and saved us many hours of wandering.

Knowledge of New Mexico waters and the flies to cast was generously shared by Bob Widgren from Los Pinos Fly Shop. We thank him for his friendship and support.

We are grateful to Jim Belshaw, who invested his considerable wordsmithing ability to convert our ragged prose into readable text.

And we thank Luther Wilson and the UNM Press for allowing us to put this obsession with rivers into a book we can share with you.

Introduction

Precious Water ONE FINAL DROP of rain from a passing thunderstorm falls on a large chunk of granite that sits on a hillside. The drop slowly slides down the damp, grainy surface. It gathers volume and momentum as it succumbs to the pull of gravity.

For a moment, it hangs on the edge of a fissure on the boulder. It has enough mass to break the grip of friction and falls like a rock-wall climber who has lost a handgrip and drops down to a scrub oak leaf. The lobbed leaf funnels the water, combining it with a myriad of other drops on the shiny skin of the foliage. It slips to the base of the leaf stem and then descends to the ground.

There is enough moisture at the base of the plant to create a small rivulet that follows a crevice in the soil to a low spot that captures more streaming trickles from other directions.

After mixing with other flows, the rill gets stronger and larger as it gains speed through an eroded ditch lower on the hillside. The stream of water flows into a larger freshet and now constitutes surface runoff. The streamlet gathers volume and velocity with each descending yard.

Within a few hundred feet, the little waterway dumps into a permanent creek that cascades down from this canyon, and eventually, after meeting other small creeks, flows into a full-sized river.

Surface water in New Mexico is a precious commodity. Cold surface-water streams that can support trout are even more rare. Most of New Mexico's streams and rivers are near roadways and developments. It is a challenge to find pristine and quiet places in which to fish for trout.

This book displays places in this state that are beautiful and accessible to you. Fly-fishing has a beauty, grace, and reward of its own. And the flies are works of art.

As anglers, we consider ourselves capable. We know how to fly fish. We are fly tiers who appreciate the artistic side of that endeavor. We love the places to fish for trout in New Mexico. We combine the science and skill of fly-fishing with the artistic beauty of the flies and place. We hope you enjoy the journey.

The photos of the forty-nine streams of New Mexico capture the allure of each place. The text captures a slice of time in the fly fishing experience. A close-up shot of the fly used in the story reveals the elegance of imitation.

We hope you visit each of these streams and find the joy we found in bringing them to these pages.

This book can be used in a variety of ways.

You can use it in your relaxing moments—visiting the rivers of New Mexico through words and photographs.

You can dream of a warm summer's day of fishing while a winter storm rages outside the walls of your home.

You can search out New Mexico waters to explore during your next outing.

You can find a river that a friend told you about and explore it on these pages before making the trip.

Enjoy the journey; it's half the fun of getting there.

Animas River

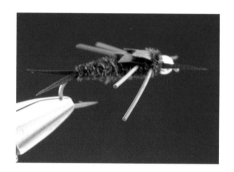

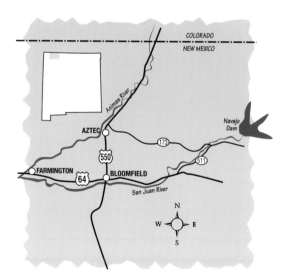

THE ANIMAS RIVER begins with its headwaters high in Colorado's San Juan Mountains and enters New Mexico south of Durango as a full-fledged river. It flows south along Highway 550 through Aztec, New Mexico, joining the San Juan River near Farmington. Along its banks several Indian pueblo ruins are available for exploring the history of this region.

The town of Aztec developed a riverside recreation area where you can access the river. There are numerous raft-and-canoe launch-and-take-out sites for your convenience.

North of Aztec the river flows through farmland, ranches, and small communities. Fishing access is limited but available.

The best time to fish the Animas is early spring before the high-mountain snowmelt swells the river with cold, off-color water; or early summer right after runoff subsides. Summer's sun warms the river rapidly, which makes it more conducive to swimming and rafting than fishing.

The river can be carefully waded when the water is not running too high. Use streamers such as Muddler Minnows to ply the deeper holes behind in-stream boulders. Twitch the fly as it tumbles into the deeper spots. Or you can prospect the runs with a double-nymph rig with a Bead Head Peacock Stone trailing a smaller caddis larva fly. Cast upstream and let the combo dead drift.

CLEAR, COLD WATER flowing over golden, moss-covered boulders gives the Brazos River bed a uniform caramel hue. This color is in stark contrast to the rich green vegetation and dark slate canyon walls that border the river. It is a stunning landscape.

In the fall you may be treated to crisp, cool mornings that give way to warm, sunny afternoons under crystalline autumn skies. There is no better time to be in the New Mexico mountains than Indian summer.

Fall trout have a sense of urgency. With the water temperatures dropping, they instinctively recognize that food will soon be less plentiful. Fall triggers them to feed with enthusiasm. Brown and rainbow trout voraciously attack both the dry fly and the dropper when this rig is fished along the seam between fast current and slow, flat water.

The many cabins that border this river limit access. However, the property owners' association and New Mexico Game and Fish have provided a fine fishing easement and access. There is about a mile and a half of river that you can hike along and fish, but the area is inconvenient as a picnic stop.

The Brazos River is a beautiful stream to visit anytime, but autumn is special in this part of New Mexico.

Just north of Tierra Amarilla on US 64/84 turn east onto NM 512. Drive about eight miles to the fishing easement access.

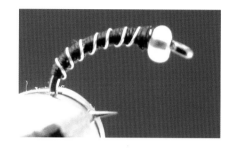

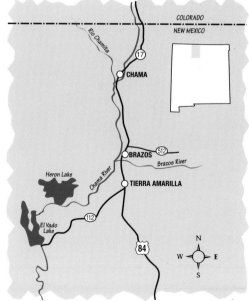

Cabresto Creek

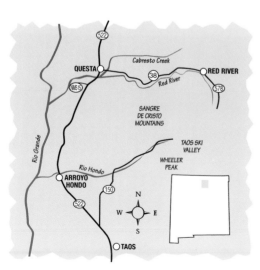

TWO HUNDRED YEARS ago prospectors in search of gold and silver traipsed up and down the canyons of the Sangre de Cristo mountain range staking claims on their hopes and dreams of riches. Dragging their gear and perhaps a donkey, they would trudge through brush and dust in search of the earth's hidden treasure.

Today we search for different treasures: mountain air, solitude, natural beauty, and trout that swim in clear, cool streams. Trudging has given away to motorized transportation. A great place to explore just north of the town of Taos is an often-overlooked little jewel of a stream called Cabresto Creek.

Headwaters trickle into Cabresto Lake and then tumble down the hillside to the confluence with Sawmill Creek. Even together, these two water sources don't create a very large stream. Willows, alders, and narrow-leaf cottonwoods form a canopy over the watercourse, making it a challenge to fish.

As you work your way carefully up this creek, make many flick-casts with a buoyant dry fly like a Yellow Humpy. A flick-cast is best made with a short leader (usually under six feet), a seven- to eight-foot fly rod and just a few feet of fly line out of the tip-top of the rod. Use short rolls of the wrist to flick the fly to likely places in the current. This is a great way to get the fly from spot to spot without getting hung up in the foliage. The number of fish available in this creek will surprise you. These are not large trout, but there are browns and rainbows up to a foot long.

Because this little stream is surrounded by more popular fishing destinations, it doesn't get a lot of angling pressure. It is a delightful place for a picnic lunch or an afternoon's fishing for golden and silvery trout.

From the town of Questa, turn east onto State Road 38 a few hundred yards, then turn north onto Forest Road 134, which parallels Cabresto Creek.

WHEN YOU VISIT Cañones Creek, which flows from the Jemez Mountains northward and then runs into El Vado Lake, the thought may occur to you that this creek is seldom traveled.

Branches hanging over both sides of the stream protect the small pools and undercut banks that hide the small trout that reside here. Thick undergrowth hampers easy maneuvering along the creek. Long-dead ponderosas that have fallen across the creek bed impede movement and casting.

As you can guess, this is a difficult stream to fish. Your rewards are small, quick, and brightly colored cutthroat trout. Dapple a small wooly worm fly at the head of deeper runs and let the fly drift down to the fish's position. These small wild trout will dart out and hastily grab it.

Or you can hike along the rugged creek-side trail and enjoy a lesser-traveled creek than you will find in most other parts of New Mexico.

Mixed conifer, aspen, and scrub oak trees surround you and whisper as mountain breezes filter through their upper branches. Pine needles and deciduous leaves carpet the trail and emit a muffled crunch with each footfall. The sweet smell of low-growing streamside mosses and grasses waft through the air.

The fishing is minimal, but if you want to hike away from the crowds Cañones Creek may be your ticket.

Access Cañones Creek by taking SR 96 across Abiquiu Dam from US 84. Turn south on FR 100 near Youngsville and drive about eight miles to a small dirt track that gets you to about a half mile from the creek.

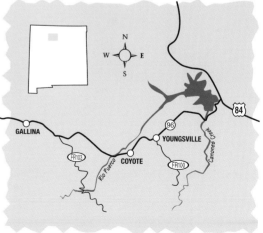

Cebolla Creek

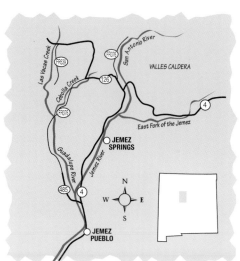

GAZE ACROSS THE meadow and you'll see gentle zephyrs creating swirling patterns atop the grasses. No sign of the stream can be seen except for an occasional stand of willows that breaks up the uniformity of the grass tops.

The Cebolla is a classic small meadow stream. It winds its sinuous way from the north end of the swale to the south. Rising above the valley floor on both sides are forested hills.

As with most meadow streams, the Cebolla is as deep as it is wide. High grasses grow right to the streamside and the tips bend over and scratch the water's surface, swaying gently with the twists and turns of the current. Fish hide in the shadows created by these grass canopies.

Angling for these meadow trout requires a different technique than in our mountain streams. It is better to not wade. Wading causes pulses through the water that fish may detect, warning them of your approach and reducing your chances of success.

Cast a dry fly, like a Goddard Caddis, onto the bending grass and let the fly topple onto the stream. Keep your fly as close to the trailing grass blades as you can. Trout will dart from their protected refuge and grab it.

The Cebolla flows from Fenton Lake. FR 376 follows the Cebolla. It crosses the stream at the top of the meadow section and again at Porter where it joins the Las Vacas to form the Guadalupe River.

WHITE, FLUFFY CLOUDS suspended in the deep-blue New Mexico sky stand in stark contrast to the yellow-tinged, brown cliffs of Mancos shale. These bluffs are the result of sand, silt, and mud deposits from ancient seas that covered this area millions of years ago.

Sediment slabs separated from the escarpment, toppled to the ground, and created giant in-stream barriers that forced the river channel to change. These deflections in watercourse carved deep cavities that harbor fish.

The Chama River flows unimpeded from the Colorado border to El Vado Reservoir. The upper stretches are a patchwork of private and public water. Eight miles of water running through the Rio Chama Wildlife area above El Vado present a medium-sized river with a nice mixture of flats, runs, riffles, and deep holes.

You can fish a dry-and-a-dropper setup to prospect this water for the browns, rainbows, and large carp that inhabit the area. Use a two-fly combination of an easy-to-see dry fly like an Irresistible for your indicator, with an attractor wet fly like the Diving Caddis. You may entice a trout to come up from the bottom to take the dry, or you can pick up subsurface feeders with the nymph. The outfit gives you twice as many opportunities to catch fish.

The roads to the river are rough, but the grandeur and beauty of this wild river running through the chiseled layers of rock are worth it.

From US 64/84 one mile north of Tierra Amarilla, turn west on to NM 112. Drive west about six miles to the first access road to the Rio Chama Wildlife Area. About one more mile west is another road to the Cottonwood Campground.

Chama River
Above El Vado

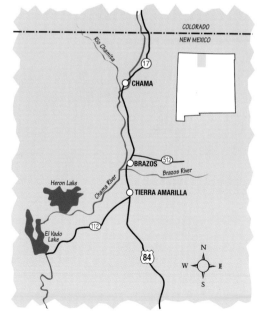

Chama River

Below the Town

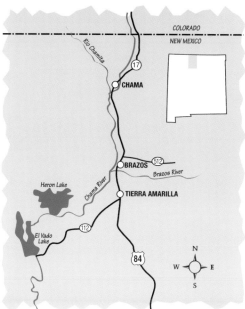

A COOL BREEZE rustles through the branches of the cottonwood trees lining the river. Some of the branches are bare of leaves and some of them have remnant yellow leaves still hanging on. Along the river you don't feel the effects of the breeze as the autumn sun warms your back.

That's the way fall is on the Chama River in northern New Mexico. The air is crisp, the sun is warm, and the fishing can be very good.

Reflections on the mirrored surface are broken by dimpling fish taking emerging insects just under the surface film. Grasshoppers abound streamside, occasionally splashing into the river after an errant flight. Cast a small Sofa Pillow dry fly to imitate the hoppers. Drop a small mayfly emerger pattern from the dry to imitate the small slate-colored nymphs hatching in the riffles.

You can easily wade up the middle of the river in hip waders in most places. This lets you cast flies to either side. Probe the deeper holes, which almost always hold one of the river's resident brown or rainbow trout.

The Chama River has a few easy public access points as a courtesy of the property owners and New Mexico Game and Fish. Spending a day on the Chama in fall provides abundant rewards.

Just south of the village of Chama on US 64/84, turn west into a public access parking lot. It is a short hike to the river.

WATER FLOWS OVER the gravel bottom, creating a long riffle that drops into a deep, dark run. At the end of the run, the stream turns right, leaving a barrel-sized eddy in the corner. A thick layer of foam covers the backwater and turns slowly with the current.

Cast a bushy dry fly, such as a Gray Wulff, into the middle of the foam mat. If one of the Cimarron's healthy brown trout is hiding under the cover, prepare for an immediate strike.

The Cimarron River emerges from under the dam that forms Eagle Nest Lake. For the first three quarters of a mile the river flows through private property. It then enters the Colin Neblett Wildlife Area where it provides miles of river to visit and fish.

The Wildlife Area offers many parking lots, pull-outs, and camping areas for visitors. It is easy access, but it is not difficult to find secluded stretches of river that you can enjoy by yourself.

The Cimarron River is a nice-sized river that is made up of smooth glides, long riffles, deep holes, and undercut banks. It is home to numerous browns and rainbows throughout the stream.

Follow US 64 from Eagle Nest Lake to below the dam. The road parallels the river the entire way to Ute Park.

Cimarron River

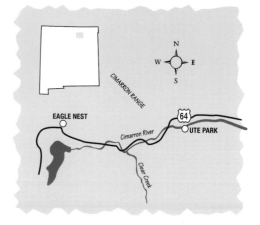

Clear
Creek

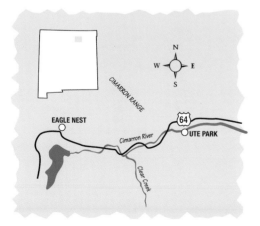

CLEAR, COOL WATER percolates down from the high country. This small creek carved a narrow, steep canyon that scoured boulders and rock faces along its course. This narrow stream bounces from rock to rock, splashes over logs and sticks, and churns under overhanging shrubs. The pockets that are created by this turbulent little creek are small, and the fish that reside in them are small. However, this little draw is rich with the sound of the creek, the rustle of leaves in the wind, and the odors of the forest.

Clear Creek is a small tributary that flows from the south and merges with the Cimarron River in the Colin Neblett Wildlife Area. You can walk up a well-maintained trail that crosses the creek many times over log bridges in the shadows of the pine, aspen, and oak.

Periodically the little stream flows over a sharp rock fracture and tumbles several feet as a waterfall. At the base of each of these falls is a plunge pool carving a deeper bowl that almost always holds fish.

Casting in small overgrown streams like this poses challenges. In many places you may have to crawl on your knees, shimmy around rock outcroppings, or wiggle between tree branches just to get your fly on the water. You may have to resort to simply dabbing your Olive Quill Spundun dry fly on the surface with your leader tip only out of the tip of your rod as it hangs over the edge of the creek. Hopefully, a small brown or cutthroat trout slashes from the shadows and grabs your dangling fly.

The trailhead for Clear Creek is just off the pavement of US 64 in about the middle of the Colin Neblett Wildlife Area below Eagle Nest Lake.

THE SMALL CREEK meanders from one side of the canyon to the other. The stream trickles over gravel beds creating long riffle-runs. Water splashes through rock gardens, adding life-giving oxygen to the creek. At each turn the current carves a deeper hole under the grassy bank, leaving a nice spot for trout to hold. Occasionally, the riverbed glides under a stand of spruce trees that provide much-needed shade to cool the water. Comanche Creek is small and intimate water, but it flows through some of the prettiest country in the state.

Granite ridgelines form the horizon on both sides of the valley. Groups of aspen fill many of the high mountain draws—mixing a lighter shade of green with the dark fir and spruce forest green. Contrast that with a typical bright blue New Mexico sky and the beauty takes your breath away.

At first glance you wonder whether this small stream holds fish. In many places you can simply step across it. However, as you approach the water, your first indication of how rich this little stream is will be the number of cutthroat trout that dart for cover.

The combination of crystal clear water and open countryside causes these fish to be especially wary of every movement in their window. When casting your small Hi-Vis Adams dry fly to these cautious trout, you must keep your profile low and your casting to a minimum. A very productive technique is to use a roll cast to reduce your exposure to the fish. Do everything you can to avoid spooking them.

From the village of Costilla on SR 522, drive east on SR 196 to the Valle Vidal area. Comanche Creek merges with the Rio Costilla at Comanche Point.

Comanche Creek

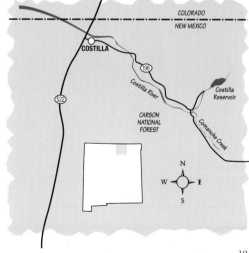

Cow
Creek

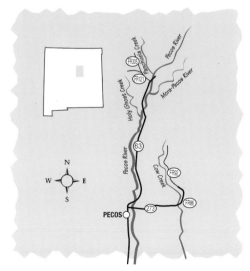

WHERE ONCE STATELY stands of pine, fir, and aspen trees covered the hillside, now barren and charred trunks remind us of a devastating forest fire that ravaged through the Cow Creek drainage. Dark spires rise in stark contrast to the rich greens of a wide variety of new vegetation.

The immediate aftermath of a catastrophic fire mars the landscape and causes complex problems to the stream's drainage area. Temperatures on the forest floor increase from the lack of leafy shade; the stream is choked with ash carried by runoff, and the fish and insect population in the river become distressed.

Over longer periods, land and rivers make a remarkable recovery. New plants and trees regenerate, grasses restore underlying sod, which stabilizes the soil against runoff, and the fish and insects become reestablished through stocking and colonization. The landscape, although very different from its original state, has unique and unusual beauty.

Large numbers of lifeless streamside trees have fallen into and across Cow Creek. These entanglements form a variety of logjams that divert and back up the stream's flow, resulting in deeper pools and runs. Water rushes from between the sticks and logs, scouring deep troughs that hold fish.

There is easy access along this river for camping, picnicking, and angling. Fishing this creek demands that you put your fly tight into the woody lies between branches. Cast your fly into the turbulent water as it's dispatched through the logjams and converts to flatter water. Trout dart from the white water, pluck your Elk Hair Caddis from the surface, and dive back down to the bottom. Your reactions had better be quick.

Access Cow Creek from FR 86 just east of the village of Pecos. Drive north through private property and enter the National Forest.

COOL, CLEAR WATER flows across and around granite boulders before it slides over the edge of the precipice and plunges seventy feet to the pool below. Jemez Falls is one of the rare waterfalls on a New Mexico stream. From a picnic area that boasts tables and bathrooms it is an easy walk on a well-maintained trail to see this beautiful waterscape.

Families frolic along the shore, people photograph friends in the spray, and visitors swim in the plunge pool. This is one of the nicest places to turn a warm, sunny summer day into a refreshing treat.

The East Fork of the Jemez has its headwaters in the Valles Calderas and has mostly public access from the La Concha picnic area down to the falls. Below the falls, it winds through a deep canyon before merging with the Jemez River at Battleship Rock, which is another access point to the canyon.

Hiding behind every rock and along its willow-lined banks, brown trout abound in this river. High-floating terrestrial dry flies like a Yellow Madam X will coax these fish into slashing strikes. You must fish short lines with just the leader on the water's surface to react quickly enough to hook these speedy fish.

In an area that attracts many visitors due to its proximity to the state's major population centers, the East Fork of the Jemez offers miles of river where you can find seclusion.

NM 4 runs through Jemez Springs and then northeast from the village of La Cueva along the southern border of the Valles Calderas.

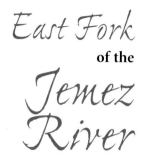

East Fork
of the
Jemez River

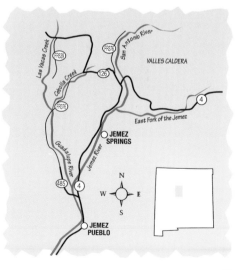

Embudo River

IF YOU HAVE an adventurous spirit, a four-wheel drive vehicle with a driver who is not faint of heart, and you're in pretty good shape, then the Embudo offers rewards not easily found in New Mexico.

Upstream the Santa Barbara and the Rio Pueblo merge on Picuris Pueblo land to form a nice-sized trout stream. The river carves its way through one of the most beautiful granite canyons in the Southwest. Swirling layers of rock form walls that the sinuous river winds between. Long, gentle runs merge into steep, noisy, cascading water that falls into deep plunge pools hiding trout in every section. This stream flows 400 feet below the canyon rim, so on most days you will have it to yourself.

Caddis flies abound in this river. Subsurface rocks covered with larvae layer the streambed. Clouds of adults in mating swarms fill the air just above the flowing water. The stream provides ideal conditions for a dry/dropper fishing setup. Use a tan Para-Caddis for your floating fly with a Bead Head Pheasant Tail as your dropper. Start at the tail-out of a run and work your way all the way up to the plunge pool at the top.

The bottom of the canyon is fairly easy to negotiate and the views are spectacular. Enjoy the day on this secluded stream, but be sure to save some energy for the climb out. You'll need it.

Access the Embudo from NM 75 west of Peñasco. Just after you leave Picuris Pueblo property there are a couple of dirt tracks that head south to the canyon rim. It's an arduous hike down from there.

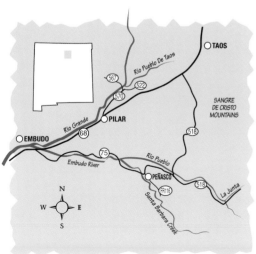

Gila River

Lower

A NORTHERN GOSHAWK soars over our heads. His short, broad wings carry him on a couple of circular passes without a wingbeat before he disappears over the eastern ridge. A dark gray water ouzel does a few deep knee bends on wetted rocks along the streamside. He looks side to side, then dives into the water in search of food. The water ouzel is the only songbird that regularly swims. Upstream, around the bend, a slate-blue kingfisher perches on an overhanging spruce limb scanning the water for an afternoon snack. Behind us, two warblers with bright yellow plumage dart from the willows on one side of the river to the other.

The lower Gila River flows through more deciduous forest than the upper reaches of the river. The river carries more water than people expect. It gently flows through level countryside with a mixture of tranquil runs and smooth flats. There are rainbow and brown trout mixed with a population of small-mouth bass. Because the river is wide open, casting a hopper-dropper setup is relatively easy. A hopper-dropper set consists of two flies. Use a grasshopper dry fly imitation because there are plenty of natural grasshoppers along the lower Gila. Then tie on a dropper fly like a small Bead Head Flash Prince Nymph to search the subsurface streambed.

This is relaxing fishing and hiking. There are no brawling, white-water cataracts. The wading is pleasant over a nonslippery gravel bottom. And once you step in and wade the river there are few tree limbs to impede your casts.

Fall is a beautiful and uncrowded time to visit the southern part of the state. You may be blessed with cool nights and warm days.

There are two ways to access the lower Gila River. From the town of Cliff, drive northeast on NM 211 to NM 293 and follow the road to the end. Then hike through the Gila Riparian Preserve to the river. Or from Cliff, drive on NM 211 to the village of Gila and then north on NM 153, which becomes more primitive as you approach the confluence of Turkey Creek and the Gila River.

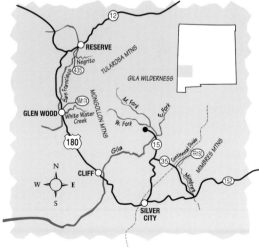

Gila River

Upper

WHEN THE WEST Fork of the Gila River meets the Middle Fork at the end of NM 15 near the Gila Cliff Dwellings National Monument, the volume of water doubles. About five miles further downstream, the East Fork of the Gila slides in and adds another third to the volume. Below this confluence, it leaves the last top-end easy access point for 25 to 30 miles.

You can walk downstream as far as you want, but be prepared to ford the stream on several occasions. Sheer rock forms the canyon walls that provide a beautiful stage for fishing and hiking.

The river changes personality many times as it wanders its course. It turns and makes gentle bends where the water is slow, flat, and reflective. In some sections the current concentrates the water flow into deep channels. At other places the river widens over a boulder-strewn bed that spawns boisterous pocket water.

Fish reside in all of these environments, but fishing for them requires you to change tactics regularly to fit the different conditions. At times you will use a high-floating dry fly to fish for feeding trout. When the river's flow is altered, you can use a small streamer to ply the deeper holding areas. On other stretches, you will want to work a small emerger or nymph pattern like the Copper Top in all the likely spots—and then you need to be ready to go back and repeat the cycle as the river varies again.

This stunning canyon is cool and lush with vegetation. You can easily get away from the crowd, find a pleasant escape from the southwestern heat, and enjoy the natural charm of this diverse habitat.

There is a parking area below the Gila Hot Springs area where the East Fork of the Gila meets the Gila on NM 15.

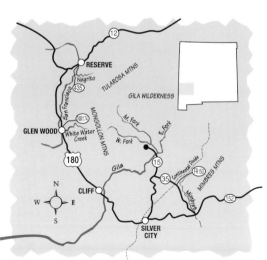

LAYERS OF GREEN hues are the most striking feature of a day on the Guadalupe River. The foliage of Virginia creeper, willow, cow's parsnip, oak, and narrow-leaf cottonwood blend with the needles of juniper, fir, and pine. These greens combine with an assortment of other plants and grasses to form a pleasant backdrop to a beautiful little mountain stream.

The Guadalupe River begins at the confluence of the Las Vacas and the Cebolla Rivers at Porter (which today is no more than a camping area). Water cascades over gentle terrain for a few miles and then courses into a gorgeous, cool, and limited-access canyon.

Another few miles downstream it plunges into a deep canyon cut with stunning rock cliffs on both sides of the river. As the road traverses this lower canyon, it is highlighted by two tunnels that were originally carved through the mountain to accommodate the trains. It is an awe-inspiring drive with breathtaking views.

A high-floating dry fly, like a Para-Hopper, cast to every rock, log, edge, and current seam can produce a fish. The number of trout that inhabit this river is surprising. On a warm spring day or a mild fall afternoon, you may get forty or fifty fish coming to your offering. They may not be large, but they are certainly rewarding.

The Guadalupe is an easy-access stream for picnics, camping and, of course, fishing.

Turn off from SR 4 below Jemez Springs onto FR 485 and follow the Guadalupe River to Porter.

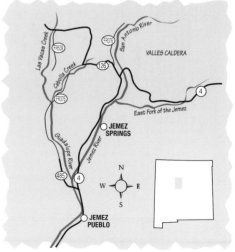

Holy
Ghost
Creek

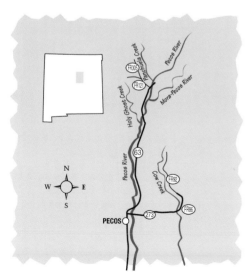

WHEN YOU FISH small streams, there is a sense of intimacy. Everything feels closer, more personal. The surroundings become your own private world.

White flower clusters of cow parsnip mixed with willows line both sides of the creek. They form curvy, floral borders to fish between. The fragrance of the flowers mingles with the aroma of trees, grass, and fresh mountain air, creating an ideal atmosphere to fish Holy Ghost Creek in the Pecos area.

As you wade the shallow stream, you can reach out to either side and touch the narrow leaves of the willows as they drag in the current. However, you must be careful with your casts or the limber branches seem to reach out and grab your fly from the air and hook it solidly in the upper twigs.

The water is pinched between rocks and deadfall debris that litters the streambed, making every cast a challenge in accuracy, but the sounds of small streams are melodious and soothe your soul. The sky seems so near, you can imagine extending your hand and capturing a patch of blue to save for yourself. It is refreshing and rejuvenating.

Everything about small streams is abbreviated. The canyons are tighter, the water flow is less, and fish are modest. Fortunately, the trout that inhabit creeks are not picky. They are considered opportunistic feeders. Often they will pounce on anything that looks "buggy." You can fish with a classic Royal Stimulator, which floats well, is easy to see, and best of all, catches these marvelous small trout.

Holy Ghost Creek is approximately ten miles north on NM 63 from the town of Pecos. It flows into the Pecos River at Terrero. There are about six miles of creek.

YOU CAN HEAR vehicles cruising by on the road over your shoulder. Sometimes, you get a glimpse of a summer cabin nestled in the trees away from the river. Always, there are reminders that you are not far from civilization.

However, in spite of all this, when you walk, fish, or just sit along the Jemez River you recognize that you are in a special place. The Jemez River is the largest stream in this vast, mountainous area that carries its name. Fish are plentiful, but skittish due to the easy access. Pullouts to park your car are numerous along the ample public water. There is a unique odor about the place, a fragrance born of volcanic soil, ponderosa and fir forest and warm, arid air. The river runs cool and clear from June through October, providing a refreshing respite.

A typical mountain freestone stream, the Jemez River tumbles between steep-graded mountain slopes over a streambed of gravel and rock. Short waterfalls create scoured-out holes that hide trout. Deeper runs that have been carved along the grassy bank conceal fish that might be larger than expected. Everywhere, trees and shrubs cast shadows on the water where trout love to hang out.

Jemez River trout do not always come easy to the angler. With a lot of people recreating in this area, the fish are wary and easily spooked into hiding. Stay back from the spot you want to present your fly and keep a low profile. A Gold Ribbed Hare's Ear is an excellent nymph to ply these waters.

SR 4 parallels the Jemez River from just above the village of San Ysidro to Battleship Rock, where you'll find the junction of the San Antonio and East Fork of the Jemez River.

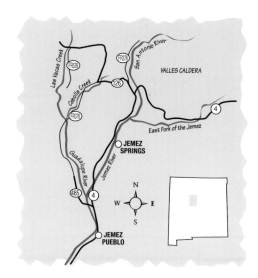

La Junta Creek

IF YOU'RE LOOKING for a nice small stream for a family camping outing, put La Junta Creek on your list. Along several miles of this gently flowing brook, wide pullouts provide grassy tree-lined spots for tents and trailers. Gray smoke drifting from family campfires, the smell of grilled hamburgers and hot dogs wafting through the mountain air, and the happy sound of kids tossing Frisbees on the grassy bank make for a pleasant way to spend a weekend in northern New Mexico mountains.

Hike up a couple hundred yards from the camping area to places where the stream ducks into the trees away from the road and you are rewarded with a pretty little mountain stream under a leafy canopy. Noises and smells fade away and you enter a tranquil environment.

As you wade up the center of the cool, clear current, cast a Red Humpy onto every crease, seam, current, and flat spot the creek offers. Small cutthroat and brown trout dart from their hiding places, grab your fly, and give you a splashy, entertaining fight. These little fish glitter in the filtered sunlight as you carefully remove the hook and let them zip back to hiding in the blink of an eye.

An afternoon on a small, intimate stream like La Junta Creek provides pleasant rewards.

Drive from Dixon on NM 75 east through Peñasco to the intersection with NM 518 heading toward Mora along the Rio Pueblo. Follow FR 76, which is a good gravel track along the creek to the north.

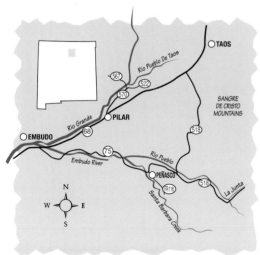

Las Vacas Creek

A HIGH, BRIGHT sun brings a blinding glare to the river's surface. A fish holds in a deep hole, snug against the gnarled roots of an overhanging willow. The shadows and branches provide good protection for the trout.

The Blue-Winged Olive dry fly must arc in with a side-armed cast to even have a chance at getting under the trailing limbs. The fly floats softly to a position a short distance upstream from the fish. After a few seconds, the twelve-inch rainbow sidles up to the fly, inspects it, and then sucks it in with a slurp. Three minutes later the fish lies in the shallows glistening in the sunlight. When it is released, it swims slowly back to its sanctuary.

An out-of-the-way stream with easy access, Las Vacas Creek falls off the radar screen for many people. It doesn't get the normal Jemez area crowds and it harbors some nice trout.

With its headwaters high in the San Pedro Peaks Wilderness, it begins as a small meadow stream teeming with cutthroat trout. It flows south and eventually merges with the Cebolla River to form the Guadalupe River.

Las Vacas Creek courses through a broad riparian valley with a diverse variety of grasses, shrubs, and trees that line the waterway. Parts of the river meander through willow-lined meadows in gentle s-curves marked by shallow runs accented by deeper, undercut banks. In other areas, it percolates over a rocky bottom that creates pools and pockets.

Along the road, there is easy access to fishing and camping opportunities.

You can drive to Las Vacas Creek on FR 126 either from the town of Cuba or over the hill from Fenton Lake. FR 539 follows the river along the lower stretch.

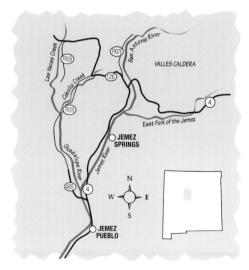

Los Pinos River

WARM WEATHER IS a tremendous time to visit one of our fine trout streams. You can picnic alongside the stream in the cool riparian shade or you can wade in the chilled water as it flows over the gravel river bottom—an ideal home to rainbow and brown trout.

Other areas of this river are a mixture of shallow riffles and deeper, darker holding water, which may harbor surprisingly large fish.

Pine trees stand in majestic groves along both banks of this stream, giving rise to its name—Rio de los Pinos—or "the river of the pines."

Most of the year this river runs clear and you can spot fish feeding gracefully on a myriad of natural insects. Toss an imitative fly into the fish's area such as a Fluttering Golden Stone and you will be rewarded with a strike.

The Los Pinos has its origin in southern Colorado and then tumbles into New Mexico below Trujillo Reservoir. Its current carves the Toltec Canyon where the Cumbres-Toltec Narrow Gauge Railroad skirts the rim. This river flows from west to east, paralleling the New Mexico/Colorado border before veering north through Antonito, Colorado, and eastward into the Rio Grande.

There are private sections on this stream, but there remains an easily accessible public area so you can enjoy this beautiful, undeveloped river.

The lower stretch of this river can be accessed on FR 103 from CO 17 at Broyles Bridge in Colorado after traversing about eighteen miles of dirt road. Easier access is from US 285 between Antonito, Colorado, and the New Mexico border over a gravel road through the village of San Antonio.

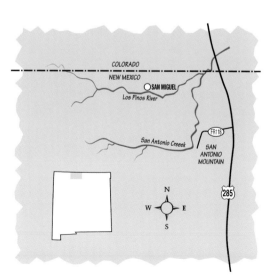

A SMALL STREAM changes the habitat of the valley through which it flows. This is especially true when it courses through a high-desert environment that is typical in many parts of New Mexico.

The riparian zone becomes rich with life different from the surrounding arid background. Inhabitants and vegetation change. A more diverse group of aquatic and terrestrial insects abound. Birds of all sizes reside along the watercourse and stray only in search of food. A variety of green grasses flourish along the bank. Water-loving deciduous trees such as narrowleaf cottonwood, willow, and alder take root in the moist soil and provide shade for the resident animals.

Small streams may harbor only small fish, but the water is a welcome oasis in an otherwise parched landscape. These fish do not attract anglers, but the dales are beautiful places to have streamside picnics and spend afternoons relaxing. The shallow water is a joy to explore, and it can reveal self-supporting micro-ecosystems that are both interesting and beautiful. As an added bonus, the temperature near a small creek is a welcome respite from the heat of the exposed countryside.

The Mimbres Creek on the southeast edge of the Gila National Forest is a tantalizing and enjoyable little stream. Its headwater begins in the upper reaches of the Black Range, flows in a generally southwest direction into the basin near the village of Mimbres, and then seeps back into the earth never to reach the sea.

Mimbres Creek flows along NM 35, but is really nice upstream, which is reached by driving about eight miles up FR 150 to the Cooney turnoff. It is very passable dirt road down to the stream in dry conditions.

Mimbres Creek

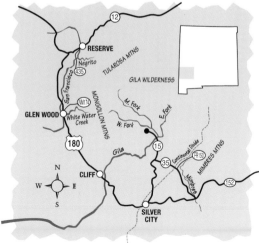

Mora-Pecos River

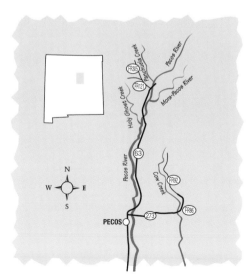

SMALL STREAMS LIKE this harbor a surprising number of fish. They hole up in nearly every nook and cranny waiting for food to drift their way.

Rays of sunshine filtered by streamside willows create intermittent sun and shadow striping on the surface of the stream. The white wing of the Parachute Adams dry fly appears to go on and off like a small beacon as it floats from dark to light and back to dark again. Small brown and rainbow trout dart from their camouflaged hiding places on the bottom and greedily take the fly in splashy rises. These Mora-Pecos fish are feisty but easy to land.

Small streams create casting challenges, as well. Sometimes you must bend at the waist and cast sideways around the limbs of drooping willows. At other times, you have to reach through branches and over rocks to just dabble your fly into tight spots. You may have to drop to your knees to flick a cast under overhanging branches. On occasion, the treetops grow over the stream creating a tunnel to cast through. And there are even stretches that open up so that you can cast normally.

The east end of the Mora-Pecos campground is a good place to park. However, the lower section gets a lot of traffic. As in many areas, the farther you walk away from the crowd, the more the river becomes pristine and secluded and fishing improves. This stream is a classic example of the 80/20 fishing rule. If you walk twenty minutes, you will be separated from 80 percent of the people.

You can easily access the Mora-Pecos from the campground on NM 63 where the Mora flows into the Pecos River about 2.5 miles north of the village of Tererro. The trail begins at the east end of the campground.

FORD THE SMALL stream in your vehicle, crunching over solid, gravely bottom before parking in the shade of a narrow-leaf cottonwood grove. After donning your fishing paraphernalia, the first thing you notice is the quiet. Only steps away, Negrito Creek flows by quietly, hardly creating a sound.

The Negrito is a continuous series of beaver ponds stacked one after another. Just a quiescent trickle of water seeps out from between the sticks and mud of a two-foot-high beaver dam. Behind the structure, in this minimally sloped riverbed, still water backs up for two hundred yards. When you reach the head of one of these lakelets, where you can discern flowing water, there is another stick-dam creating another placid pond.

Fishing beaver ponds is challenging. The flat surface telegraphs every top disturbance. A fly line landing is like a rock hitting your windshield at 60 miles per hour—it causes the fish to flinch.

If fish are feeding on the quiet surface, they are usually cruising. The trick is to cast a small dry fly, like a Ginger Quill Spundun, to a position you imagine is ahead of where you think the fish is going. By leading the fish, you can reduce fly line disruption. After your fly has floated on the water for a few seconds, you can really entice strikes with subtle twitches of the fly. Feeding trout can't resist this technique.

If there are no fish perceptibly feeding, you can ply the deeper water with a Damselfly Nymph. Cast and give short strips to mimic the natural insect's action. When a trout takes this fly, it is usually with gusto.

Negrito Creek is accessed by turning east onto Negrito Creek Road from NM 435 just south of Reserve.

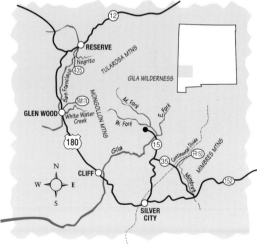

Panchuela Creek

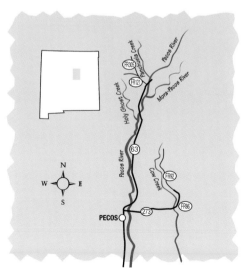

PECOS WILDERNESS IS headwaters to many northern New Mexico streams. A lot of the smaller ones never leave the boundary perimeter. A pretty stream that begins high on Pecos Baldy and eventually flows into the Pecos River is Panchuela Creek.

This medium-sized creek glides between stands of fir and pine trees and through a serene and beautiful canyon away from the crowds. From the parking area there are a few walk-in camping areas with shelters, tables, and fire pits. The streamside trail climbs over a rocky ridge and then drops back down to the creek. Within a short hike, you are in the wilderness area.

The riparian area is a rich, loamy soil heavy with moisture. This environment is a productive growing medium for forest flora. Plants of every shape and shade of green carpet the stream's banks. Bright wild-flowers stretch their stalks higher than the foliage and add color to the scene. White mushrooms hang on the shaded edges of long-ago-harvested ponderosa pine stumps. Small ruddy-brown mushroom caps peek out from detritus stacked up under trees.

Fishing this creek is fairly easy. In many places the stream widens, making casting and approach to nice holes handy. Numerous pools are deep with steady current. Use a dry/dropper setup with a Royal Wulff and an attractor dry fly with a Flash-Back Pheasant Tail Nymph as your dropper.

With the combination of a babbling creek, the captivating elegance of mountain scenery, and a buffer to the crowded campgrounds, Panchuela Creek is a prize.

Take SR 63 to Tererro north of the village of Pecos and then FR 121 to FR 305 north of Cowles.

THE BUOYANT RED Quill dry fly coasts along with the current, bouncing from rock to rock in a riverine pinball game. The river's circulation swoops the fly around stones and deposits it in slack water that forms downstream from the protrusion. When the fly pauses for an instant, a lurking brown trout rockets up, grabs it, and dives back down to its hiding place.

These stream-born trout take a fly with dazzling speed. You must be quick and assertive when setting the hook. Without allowing the fly line to slip through the guides, promptly lift the rod tip to set the hook securely. Trout that inhabit this type of stream can eas-ily cause you to miss the hookup and leave you empty handed and frustrated.

Browns in this part of the Pecos River are a light golden-olive with bright orange spots. Although they are not large, they are a joy to catch.

Rocky slopes rise steeply above both sides of this freestone stream creating a box canyon stretch of river that is easily accessible from the bottom near Tererro, as well as from the top end near Cowles. The river between these two entry points is about five miles of secluded water. The Pecos area attracts a lot of people, but this section offers tremendous views and vista of classic New Mexico mountain scenery with fishing and hiking away from the congestion.

As it runs through the bottom of the canyon, the river is relatively open and easy to wade. The openness allows for an unrestricted casting stroke, which reduces snags. Wild flowers bloom along both sides, creating blankets of resplendent color that add to the angling pleasure.

Drive about 15 miles north on NM 63 from the town of Pecos to reach the lower section of the box canyon.

Pecos River

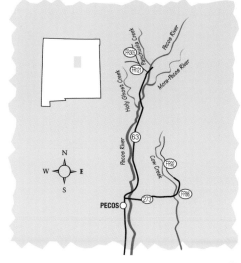

Red River

Lower

TREES AND SHRUBS along the stream swell with leaf buds. Spring is just around the corner. But snow patches still persist in the shadows on the north-facing hillside.

New Mexico's March weather is forever changing. Within just a couple of hours on any given day you may have an overcast sky filled with agitated clouds that are displaced with partly sunny periods. Then cool winds might bring rain and snow. And then it can go back to sunny again before the day is done.

With unsettled spring weather, it is wise to delay the beginning of your day. You can spend an afternoon on a pretty stretch of water that is easily accessed by trail downstream from the Red River Fish Hatchery. Picnic tables are tucked into wooded areas along the river. There is also a fishing pond adjacent to the parking area.

The water in the Red River runs clear and cool this time of year, but carries a blue-green–tinged hue as a result of the headwaters percolating through mine tailings.

During the middle of the day, fish take small subsurface flies such as a RS2 Flash Green Nymphs. As the water warms up in late afternoon, trout can be caught on dry flies such as Elk Hair Caddis or Parachute Adams.

Late winter fishing does not produce fast and furious action, but you can catch enough to keep it interesting. Red River comes with a solitude bonus this time of year as well. You won't find summer's crowded stream. Often the river belongs to you alone, or at most a handful of others.

Drive north from Taos on US 64 to NM 522. About three miles south of Questa turn west on NM 515 to the Red River Hatchery. The trail begins at the west end of the hatchery.

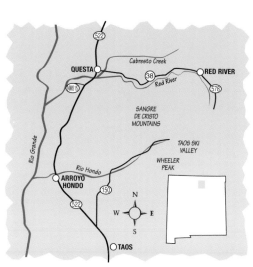

THE TOWN OF Red River is a hub of summer and winter tourist activity. The Red River itself flows through the center of town and offers recreational fishing in places. However, to really appreciate the wild fishery, drive upstream from the town to where the river cuts through a deep canyon and the road rises to the ridgeline. It is special fishing regulation water that is easily accessed from either the top or the bottom of the canyon, but it is treacherous to attempt to scramble down in the middle. The river bottom is fairly easy to get around or across and offers unique solitude in this popular and populated area.

Even though this stream does not run along the road in the canyon section, over the season, it gets substantial fishing pressure. The fish are wary and selective. Caddis flies may be swarming in the air and ovipositing eggs on the water's surface, piquing the fish's attention. Just prospecting for fish can be productive, but often they will not take your fly. If you find a fish or a group of fish feeding in a run, be patient. Work your Yellow Bulletproof Caddis in the area over and over. Sometimes your fly just needs to match the fish's rhythm of feeding as well as be the correct pattern. Persistence pays off.

The Red River Canyon is a beautiful stretch of river with spectacular scenery and solitary fishing.

Take US 64 north from Taos and continue north of NM 522 when US 64 turns west. Turn east on NM 38 through the town of Red River and then veer off on NM 578 to the Red River Canyon.

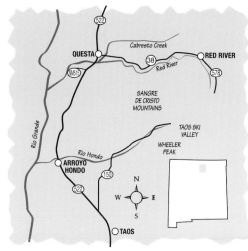

Rio Chamita

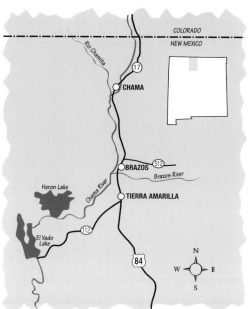

THIS LITTLE CREEK wanders its course on the northern New Mexico mountains. It begins as a trickle high up on the shoulder of Chama Peak, which straddles the New Mexico/Colorado border. It meanders around boulders and rocks. It swerves and twists around fallen trees. It cuts under grassy banks. And it gains additional volume and strength as it flows downward.

The Rio Chamita is still a small creek where it winds its way through the Edward Sargent Wildlife Area northwest of Chama. But in New Mexico, small is not a bad thing. It is more the norm.

In the lower sections, this creek bends and turns through flat bottomland. The result is a quiet and friendly creek. Cast a RS2 Gray next to the undercut banks and under the overhanging shrubs. Mostly, small trout will grab the fly.

Occasionally a fish of over twelve inches will surprise you. Your presentation must be delicate with small flies and thin, gossamer leaders in this intimate stream.

The wildlife area is also a tremendous place to hike and enjoy the mountainous wide-open spaces, song birds and waterfowl. The blue sky is as captivating as it is expansive.

Treat yourself to a day on the Rio Chamita.

From the town of Chama, turn west off NM 17 on First Street and then turn north onto Pine Street to access the parking lot for the Sargent area.

WATER CHURNING OVER the v-dam gouges a large, deep hole on the downside. Below, the stream bubbles and then forms into multiple current seams. When you work a dry/dropper setup from the tail-out to the log vee, feisty trout may grab either the floating hopper pattern or a green Copper John Nymph.

Throughout the upper reaches of the Rio Costilla below Costilla Reservoir, this long series of v-dams has greatly improved the fishery. The Rio Costilla was a fast-flowing meadow stream with occasionally good holding water, but the addition of the dams—two logs making a vee pointing into the current—has created abundant, ideal protection for trout.

The upper Rio Costilla is a wide-open high mountain meadow stream with frequent stands of spruce and willow bordering the river. The Rio Costilla is easily accessible with SR 196 running along side it. This stretch of river is in the Valle Vidal area and is stunning it its beauty.

The lower stretch of the river after its confluence with Comanche Creek is a little larger. It also runs parallel to SR 196 with many grassy pullouts to park, camp, or picnic.

The river in this lower section varies between narrow, fast, tree-lined runs and flat, wide-open meadows with grassy banks and deep undercuts. Cutthroat and rainbow/cutthroat hybrid trout dominate this section.

From the village of Costilla on SR 522, drive east on SR 196 to the Valle Vidal area. The Rio Costilla merges with Comanche Creek at Comanche Point.

Rio Costilla

Rio del Medio

THE TRAIL LEADS steadily downward at a gentle grade. Stark remains of charred tree trunks give the hiker an eerie sensation. Switchbacks dominate the path's descent to the canyon bottom and a cool, green riparian area awaits you along the Rio del Medio.

There is little fire evidence in the streamside foliage except for a few fallen trees that leave soot on your hands and clothes if you brush against them as you pass. The water, clear over a cobbled bottom, churns around boulders and rock slabs, creating a pleasant and relaxing audible background to your fishing or hiking.

The Rio del Medio is a medium-size stream that in many places provides open water and open vegetation so that casting is not too precarious. Little brown trout lay waiting for floating insects to pass their spot. Late in the season, grasshoppers crawl on tall grasses and shrubs and launch into buzzing flights across the stream. Cast a good grasshopper imitation like a Stalcup Hopper to every part of the stream. Let it splat onto the water's surface to stimulate strikes from these feisty wild fish.

This canyon is a mountain in reverse. The high ridge where you start your walk is arid soil covered with chamisa and cactus. When you get to the bottom, it's a mixed conifer, willow, and oak forest. The Rio del Medio is a delightful canyon river with one drawback: at the end of a day you have to hike back up the trail about 500 vertical feet to reach your vehicle.

To reach the Rio del Medio, turn on to NM 503 north of Pojoaque and head for Chimayo. Just north of Cundiyo take FR 306 east to either the Borrego trailhead or the Borrego Campground to access a trail to the river.

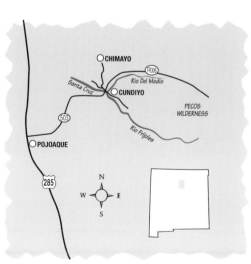

WATER CURLS AROUND jumbled rocks in the streambed. In front of the rock piles the stream's flow backs up into deeper holes with shadowed crevices. A Renegade dry fly hits the water where flow drops a foot from a flattened rock upstream. The little fly floats and flutters with the conflicting currents for a moment. Then it begins its lazy drift along the foam-line toward the tail of the pool. Just before it drops into the next basin, a feisty brown trout slashes at the fly and sinks it to the bottom with him. Small fish in this mountain stream are quicker than you imagine.

The Rio Frijoles starts as a trickle high on the shoulders of Pecos Baldy. It gathers water from small springs and side canyons as it travels down the slope, where it has carved a steep-walled canyon in its lower section that protects it from visitors, except those willing to hike past the private land or in from the top.

When you make the effort, you will find yourself in a secluded and shaded canyon, beautiful in its wildness. The cool water is refreshing to wade in as sunlight filters through the overhanging branches. Striped patterns of light and dark dance on the water's surface. This is a very nice place to spend a summer's day.

The Rio Frijoles merges with the Rio del Medio at Cundiyo to form the Santa Cruz River. You can access the stream from a trailhead at Panchuela Campground or bushwhack from the Cundiyo area. Take NM 503 north of Pojoaque east to the village of Cundiyo.

Rio Frijoles

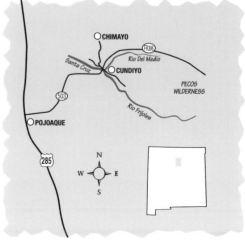

Rio Grande

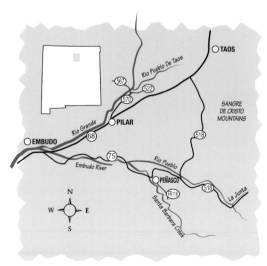

MOST OF THE snow and rain that falls on New Mexico soil ends up in the Rio Grande. This river is one of the west's major waterways with its headwaters in Colorado and its mouth in the Gulf of Mexico. This important river enters New Mexico on the northern border and exits on the south after dissecting the state.

In the northern half of the state, it is a trout stream with pike and carp mixed in. The Rio Grande is a large river by New Mexico standards. The fishing can be fickle. When the fish are on, it can be very good. When the fish are off, it is downright difficult.

The most notable feature of the Rio Grande is the Box Canyon near Taos and Questa. This spectacular gorge was created when glacial ice was melting and receding northward while the vast lava fields that covered this area were upwelling. The Rio Grande flows seven hundred feet below the rim and winds its way through dark, majestic lava cliffs. It was the first river designated under the National Wild and Scenic River Act in 1968.

The Rio Grande supports a large variety of insects, with caddis being the most plentiful. During the summer months, these insects induce the fish to feed late afternoons and into the evening up until dark. Fish move to the edges and devour the dancing adults. Fish to specific feeding fish with a Double Hackle Peacock for an evening's entertainment.

High water in spring sprouts rafters by the thousands. This river definitely deserves the Wild and Scenic moniker. It is worth visiting any time of year.

There is access along SR 68 from below Embudo to Pilar. SR 570 skirts the river from Pilar to the SR 567 Bridge. NM 522 crosses at the John Dunn Bridge at the bottom of the Box. Or you can hike down one of the trails between Questa and the Colorado border.

EVERY NEW MEXICO stream has its own personality. Each river leaves its own lasting impression. After fishing the Rio Hondo, you want to savor and store in your memory the essence of the experience.

The memorable sound of this river can be heard from the Taos Ski Area westward to the Rio Grande. As water spills over and around rocks of varied sizes, it produces a natural symphony, a unique mountain melody whose arrangement creates music that stays with you long after you have left and headed for home.

Clear water plunging over short waterfalls creates deep, resonant bass notes. The tenors arrive when the stream's flow is pinched between two rocks. The altos chime in when side sprays strike small stones along the edges. The orchestration brings a grand rhythm to the day's fishing.

Another striking feature of this beautiful little river is the color of the rocks that make up the streambed. A mixture of bright golds, browns, greens, and yellows fashion a perfect background to disguise the many brown trout that inhabit this stream.

Ply these waters with small, bushy, easy-to-see dry flies like the House-n-Lot. Since it rides high on the water and with white wings, it is very easy to see in the turbulent currents that hide trout.

A great way to spend a day is to walk along this beautiful stream catching small brown trout from every holding spot as you listen to the harmonious sounds of water cascading over rocks.

This easily accessible river is a great place to fish or just hang out enjoying lyrical mountain music.

The Rio Hondo has its headwaters above the Taos Ski Valley with NM 150 bordering it most of the way.

Rio Hondo

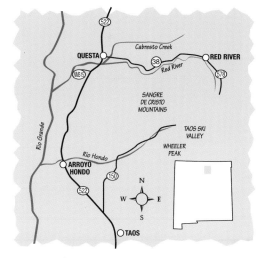

Rio Pueblo

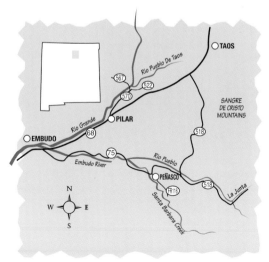

COOL, CLEAR WATER gurgles around the mangled roots of an uprooted pine tree. A deep hole filled with water replaces the vacant space once occupied by the base of a tree. It creates an ideal place to harbor trout. A Purple Haze Caddis dry fly cast into the mass of roots pauses for a moment and then falls onto the water's surface. Immediately, an energetic brown trout grabs the fly and is hooked solidly.

Even though the Rio Pueblo is easily accessible with many miles of NM 518 running parallel to it, there are still plenty of willing fish to make the experience rewarding. The streambed borders the roadside in many places. But it also meanders away from the pavement and disappears behind the trees. Sections that are the farthest away from the road and less traveled by visitors improve the angling.

With its headwaters high in the Sangre de Cristo Mountains, this cascading mountain stream drains a fairly large watershed and becomes a nice mid-sized stream. It is a nice stretch of water to fish, wade, or picnic near. It flows through a flat-bottomed valley with heavily forested banks that rise steeply on both sides of the stream. The views of the high mountain peaks form a tremendous backdrop for this lovely trout stream.

You can access the Rio Pueblo on NM 75 from Dixon east through Peñasco to the intersection with NM 518 heading toward Mora. You can also reach this junction by taking NM 68 east from Taos and merging onto NM 518.

SOME RIVERS WHISPER even when you are very near. Some rivers gurgle and murmur as they tumble through rock gardens. Some rivers churn and splash as they cascade through descending terrain. And some rivers are downright loud and boisterous as they crash their way around boulders.

The Rio Pueblo de Taos fills the air with its raucous and feverish flow as it tumbles its way through a narrow rock-strewn canyon before it plunges into the Rio Grande. From the high-desert mesas on the rim of the Rio Grande Gorge, it carves its way through lava cliffs and drops down a steep canyon of its own. The streambed is a combination of precipitous chutes that the water rushes down and gouged-out plunge pools. These pools are surprisingly deep and can hold healthy, fat brown and rainbow trout.

Even though you can nearly drive to streamside, it is still no easy feat to get to the water. You must scramble down a steep embankment of loose gravel and dirt. The climb out can be treacherous. This is not a stream for a family picnic.

Once on the river, you can boulder-hop and wedge your way around rocks larger than your vehicle. Cast a Bead Head Caddis Larva into every channeled area of the pools and the seams of the current. In many cases, you will stand on a rock in one pool and cast to the next spot upstream which may be at your eye level. This is tough fishing. However, the deep Rio Grande canyon scenery is classic New Mexico.

The easiest access is from NM 570 north out of Pilar through the Orilla Verde Recreation Area to the Taos Junction Bridge. A gravel road ends a few hundred yards at the Rio Pueblo de Taos.

Rio Pueblo de Taos

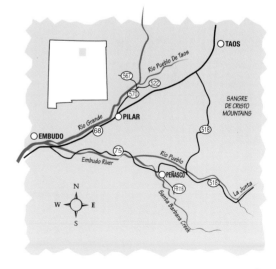

Rio Puerco

THE BUTTER-COLORED brown trout fins in the shallow clear water to hold its position. Sunlight from an afternoon sun flickers on the water as it filters through the tree branches. The fish periodically moves to one side or the other to sip an imperceptible insect from the water's surface.

The angler, hiding in the shadows below the fish, is preparing to cast a small Flash-back Prince Nymph. After just one false cast, the fish darts for cover without even giving the angler a chance.

This scenario took place on the Rio Puerco, a small stream that tumbles down the northern slopes of the Jemez Mountains. There are plenty of fish in this river, but they are extremely wary of movement.

After coursing a narrow canyon, the Rio Puerco breaks out into a beautiful mountain valley at the Rio Puerco Campground. Below this point, the river winds through mixed forest with thick vegetation growing right down to the river's edge. Fallen trees add to the angling challenge.

This is a pretty little stream to visit and get away from the crowds. You can enjoy a cool day in the shade of tall pines near a babbling brook. Take the family for a picnic. Wander up the canyon on a day-hike. And try the fishing.

There are two streams that come off the Jemez Mountains called the Rio Puerco. One heads east of Cuba and flows southwest. This one heads on the north side and flows into Abiquiu Lake.

From NM 96 between Gallina and Coyote turn south on FR 103 and drive about 10 miles to the Rio Puerco.

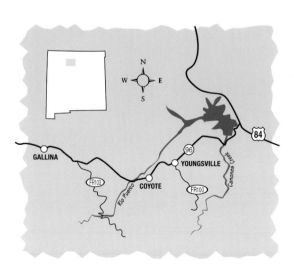

TAKE A HIKE along a streamside trail that parallels a creek. The path wanders from soft soil under grassy banks to rocky hardpan stretches next to the base of a cliff. The footpath takes you from shaded areas under verdant canopies to sunlit exposed expanses.

Marvel at the variety of trees, shrubs, and grasses that flourish in the moist environs. It's hard to imagine that many shades of green. Soak in the wonder of bright, shiny berries that adorn streamside foliage. Listen intently to birds that flutter through the willows and mixed conifer trees. You can catch a glimpse of juncos, chickadees, nuthatches, warblers, and jays that populate the riparian zone that borders the creek.

In the scope of this book, not every small brook or creek is included. But that is not to say these smaller waters are not enjoyable. It is a pleasure to walk along these murmuring creeks.

With enchanted New Mexico names such as Rito en Medio, Coñones Creek, Tecolote Creek, Agua Fria Creek, Cottonwood Creek, Redondo Creek, Guaje Creek and numerous others, these small waterways drain the mountaintops through canyons throughout the state. They can be found in every quadrant.

These diminutive streams possess mesmerizing beauty along their courses and are worth visiting and exploring. Most of them contain small brook, cutthroat, rainbow, or brown trout. However, because of their brushy, overgrown nature, they are very difficult to fish.

Search out the streams near you, explore the trails, and revel in the charms they offer. It is a rewarding way to spend a pleasant New Mexico day.

Ritos Numerosos

Ruidoso River

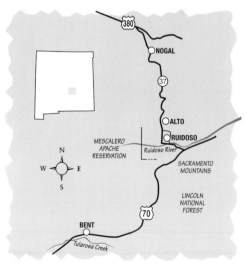

THE CITY OF Ruidoso is known more for its skiing and horse racing than it is as fishing destination. With its headwaters on the Mescalero Reservation, the Ruidoso River cascades down the hillside through Upper Canyon. It then mellows as it flows right through the middle of town paralleling Main Street.

At first you may be intimidated but still curious about fishing so near urban development. However, once you reach the clear-flowing water and begin wading and casting your fly, the sights and sounds of the town melt into the background of the rushing water.

Parts of this stream run along residential lawns and gardens that reach down to the river's edge. Sections flow through public parks and picnic areas with families eating and playing games. And there are parcels where you don't see or hear a sign of the surrounding village.

Trees tower on both sides creating a cool, shady tunnel for this small, meandering stream to flow. Portions of the creek are open and easy to cast. Other parts are overgrown in an arboreal mesh making it difficult to reach with a fly. However, when you can get a good cast into a tight spot, a brown or rainbow will dart from its hiding spot and quickly grab your Miracle Caddis.

If fishing within a town disquiets your senses, take heart. There is a special treat. When you are hungry for lunch you can climb out of the water, dine in a pleasant café on Main Street, and then return to the river for afternoon angling. No remote destination offers the angler this special bonus.

WHEN YOU LEAVE US 285 and drive west on the flat-gradient gravel road for six miles along the north shoulder of San Antonio Mountain, you might have difficulty imagining you're approaching a cool trout stream. Low brush and arid-loving critters keep their distance from your vehicle. Pronghorn look up warily and melt over the low horizon. Just ahead of you, western bluebirds flutter from bush to bush just keeping ahead of you. Meadowlarks erupt from the roadside and hustle away. Kestrels and turkey vultures soar in graceful circles far overhead. There are lava rock, dirt, low-lying shrubs, and chamisa everywhere. And no water to be seen.

You will eventually reach the rim of a canyon where you can look down on cottonwoods and willows lining a small, sinuous stream. The green, grassy banks are a welcome sight after the parched drive. After parking the car, you traipse down a sloped canyon wall, avoiding cactus with every step.

At the bottom you feel substantially cooler than you did on the ridge. San Antonio Creek is small, but it creates a comfortable and shaded oasis. The stream has carved a pretty canyon with high walls of rugged lava stone giving way to gently sloping soil and rock that eases into the flattened streambed.

Small fish are few and far between, so this is not an angler's paradise. A small Peacock Stimulator cast along the cut-banks and near fallen tree trunks may coax a strike from one of these wary fish.

San Antonio Creek is an ideal getaway for a picnic and a hike that doesn't see a lot of visitors.

Access San Antonio Creek from US 285 on to FR 118. After about six miles, you can hike down to the small stream. Or, from US 285 between Antonito, Colorado, and the New Mexico border you can drive through the village of San Antonio where the creek merges with the Los Pinos River.

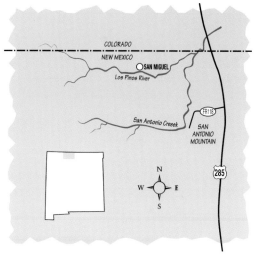

San Antonio River

Lower

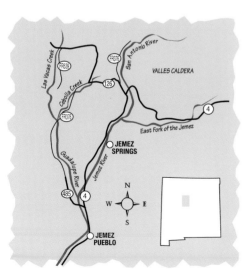

TREES LINE THE high horizon on the east side of the San Antonio canyon like sentinels. When you walk the river early in the morning, the sunlight sparkles through the Douglas fir boughs like a reflection from the facets of a diamond.

It can be mid-morning before the warming rays of the sun reach the water's surface. The waterway stays chilly, permitting the resident trout and insects to sleep in a little longer. Trout are cold-blooded critters. When cool overnight water temperatures begin to rise from the sun's warmth, fish increase their feeding pace.

The lower portion of the San Antonio River descends from one granite shelf to the next all the way down the canyon. The clear water courses over these steps creating little waterfalls at measured distances. Each additional footfall brings you to a whole new set of small, delightful pockets of water that hold the promise of trout.

The best technique here is "pickpocket" fishing. With a short line you can pop a high-riding Ginger Quill dry fly into each of these flat-water patches. Let the fly float naturally in every likely-looking location and you will be pleasantly amazed at the number of fish you can entice.

This type of prospecting for fish can be entertaining, productive, and a tremendous way to spend the day on a dazzling stretch of river.

Drive about sixteen miles north on NM 4 from San Ysidro to Battleship Rock. This is where the San Antonio and the East Fork of the Jemez meet. There are four miles of river between this point and La Cueva at the intersection of NM 4 and NM 126. Much of this section is known as Dark Canyon.

ON SUMMER AFTERNOONS, once the sun has warmed the earth, grasshoppers crawl, jump, and fly in every part of the grassy fields that border the upper San Antonio River. Countless errant hoppers tumble onto the stream where ravenous trout inhale them off the surface. The telltale concentric rings of the rise reveal the position of the trout.

Fish wolf down the Turk's Tarantula dry fly, a noted, low-riding, small grasshopper imitation. Keep your profile low when fishing because this meandering meadow river is devoid of trees along its shore. The trout are wary and vigilant for two-legged, stick-waving predators. On any pastureland stream, trout tuck up beneath undercut banks for sanctuary.

The upper San Antonio is one of two streams that originate in the Valles Calderas. The other is the East Fork of the Jemez. The Valles Calderas is the 15-mile wide, million-year-old collapsed volcano that is so imposing that it can be observed from outer space.

Rich in nutrients as a result of the volcanic cache-basin, the San Antonio supports the type of aquatic vegetation that harbors a diverse variety of aquatic and terrestrial insects. Insects are the staple of a trout's diet.

This genre of sinuous meadow stream is not common to New Mexico. We must protect and cherish the few we have. The views are spectacular and the mountain air is habit-forming.

To access the upper San Antonio River, drive approximately twenty miles north on NM 4 from San Ysidro through Jemez Springs to La Cueva at the intersection with NM 126. Drive west about two miles to FR 376. Turn north and drive about four miles on the dirt road to the access parking area.

San Antonio River
Upper

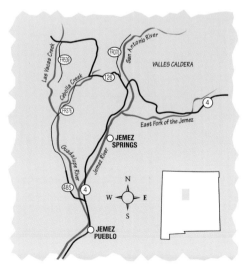

San Juan River

Summer

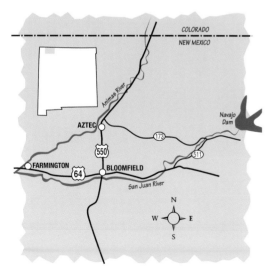

WATER CHURNS FROM the bottom of the dam that holds back Navajo Lake. It comes out cool and clear, spawning the San Juan River. The volume of water and constant temperature that hovers around fifty degrees creates an ideal habitat to grow large trout. These factors combined with special fishing and harvest regulations make this river one of the premier trophy trout fisheries in the Southwest.

The San Juan River flows through a flat-bottomed arid valley where the river is wide with split channels that provide a myriad of angling opportunities. And it needs it. The San Juan River is one of the most popular angling destinations in New Mexico.

With wide-open runs and banks lined with cottonwood, willow, and tamarisk, there are numerous fishing spots throughout the valley. The top three-and-three-quarter miles downstream from the dam have been designated for flies and lures with single barbless hooks only. However, with a little guidance, even novice anglers can successfully catch fish.

San Juan trout are your reward. They grow big and strong. They are accustomed to anglers, so they do not always come easily to your fly. Ply the channels and riffles with a Baetis Hackle Wing dry fly. When the fish are feeding on the surface, it is often to midges. Use an emerger pattern that imitates these most prolific insects on the river.

Blue skies dominate this region and you might be treated to the sight of a soaring bald eagle as it cruises the river valley.

The San Juan River attracts many visitors because of the big water, big fish, and big fun.

You access the San Juan from US 64 in Bloomfield east to SR 511, which parallels the river to Navajo Dam. From Aztec, take SR 173 east, which merges with SR 511.

ICE CRUNCHES UNDER each footstep as you work your way along the marshy trail from the road to the river on winter mornings. Trees are leafless, grasses are straw-colored and crunchy from the overnight frost, your breath is visible when you exhale, patches of bankside snow submit to the sun's warming rays as drops fall into the river, the sky is clear, and the sun is bright.

The San Juan River in the northwest corner of the state is one of the country's premier tail water fisheries. Tail water is the stretch of river that is immediately downstream from a dam. Water is siphoned from the reservoir's depths, providing cool and consistent temperatures. This trout-friendly environment is rich with aquatic insects that provide a steady, year-round food source. This allows the fish to grow twelve months of the year. Anglers catch many trout that are twenty inches and longer in this fabled river.

This river can get overpopulated with anglers, but winter weather thins the crowds so you can find sections of the river for yourself. An ideal way to fish this river during the colder months is with two nymphs. Use a larger, weighted fly that sinks quickly to the bottom and draws a smaller nymph like a Red Midge Larva down with it as a dropper. You will catch fish on both flies, but most will be hooked on the smaller one.

Winter is a pleasant time to be on the San Juan River. A sunny day warms your body. There are no pesky, biting insects. And, there are plenty of big, strong fish.

Drive east on US 64 from Bloomfield about 12 miles to SR 511 towards Navajo Dam. There are many river access points along an eight-mile stretch.

San Juan River
Winter

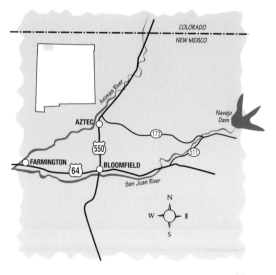

Santa Barbara Creek

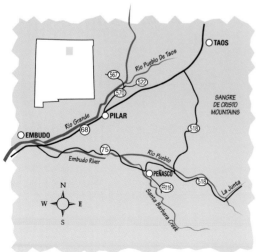

THE SANTA BARBARA campground is bustling with activity. Trailers and campers fill spaces at every conceivable angle. Tent campers have rain-fly-covered picnic tables strewn with gear. Families walking their dogs circle the service road. Kids splashing each other in the stream fill the air with giggles. All kinds of family sounds reverberate among the pines.

It's an easy walk from the campground to a truly wild and beautiful mountain valley. Towering aspen trees stand on both sides of the trail creating a leafy canopy. Fir and spruce trees climb up the draws along the hillside. Ferns carpet the shaded meadow bordering the walking track. Small springs seep from the ground and muddy the trail in spots. The smell of fresh, damp foliage fills the nostrils.

It's amazing that you can walk twenty minutes from a crowded, public area and arrive in pristine surroundings, clear mountain air, and solitude.

The Santa Barbara Creek flows over a streambed turned golden from dissolved minerals in the water. It glows brightly in the sunshine as you walk along its bank. Clear water percolates around boulders and rocks. Fish hide in a multitude of places.

Flick a Yellow Stimulator into every seam, riffle, run, and flat spot to catch feisty cutthroat and brown trout. These brightly colored fish cap off a delightful afternoon in the mountains.

You reach the Santa Barbara Campground from NM 75 in Peñasco to the junction with NM 73. In about 1.5 miles, turn left onto FR 116. It is about four miles to the camping area. The trail to seclusion begins at the east end of the campground.

THERE ARE NOT many places in New Mexico where a paved road crosses a river at its only place of access, especially when that river then plunges into a rugged canyon reachable by trail. The Santa Cruz River is such a place. The Rio del Medio flows in from the northeast and the Rio Frijoles flows in from the southeast with their confluence just east of the NM 503 bridge. They form the Santa Cruz. The canyon, with coarse, jagged cliffs winds for about a mile before it spills into Santa Cruz Reservoir.

This river flows through terrain that is only about seven thousand feet in elevation with the surrounding countryside dominated by arid high desert. The stream, having percolated from the peak of Pecos Baldy, runs cool and clear over gravel and rock bottom.

Periodically, along the course of the stream, large boulders have tumbled from bordering ridges and formed large, deep pools that harbor trout.

Most of this stream is easy to walk along or in the edges in waders, except that some of the holes are over four feet deep. The best way to fish this stream is to walk down the trail and fish your way back up. Wading the edges of the stream and flicking your Poly Patriot dry fly into every current and seam pays dividends. Pay special attention to the back eddies. This is where some of the larger fish reside.

Take NM 503 north of Pojoaque east toward Chimayo. In the village of Cundiyo, park in the lot next to the highway bridge.

Santa Cruz River

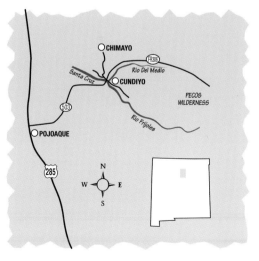

Tularosa Creek

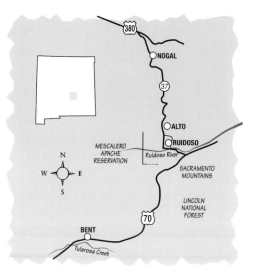

WHEN YOU'RE DRIVING on US 70 between the desert town of Tularosa and the Sacramento Mountains, there is little in your view that makes you think of a trout stream. The landscape is dotted with mesquite bushes, chamisa shrubs, cactus, and a few juniper trees. Between these widely spaced plants there is dirt—lots of parched, hot dirt. Then the highway unexpectedly crosses a deep, healthy-green, foliage-filled arroyo. This glimpse provides a hint of what is cached at the bottom of the sandstone canyon.

Tularosa Creek begins as a full-blown spring creek on the Mescalero Reservation and flows in a south-western direction through the village of Bent and then downward into the desert flats above the town of Tularosa where it seeps into the sand and disappears.

From the highway crossing to the Reservation boundary you will find an unexpected gem of a trout stream that runs cool and clear. It is small, intimate, contains browns and rainbows, and appears to be rarely fished.

The real joy of this little stream is the micro-ecosystem it creates. While the sun beats on the surrounding hillsides, narrow-leaf cottonwoods, cottonwoods, pines, and willows form a green canopy. Underneath, the stream is bordered by grassy banks that grow right down to the water's edge. Flowers and bushes abound and the temperature feels twenty degrees cooler than outside the canyon.

Fish with a short line, plying the deeper holes with a Flash Pheasant Tail Nymph, and be rewarded with small, quick, and feisty trout that don't see many anglers.

Tularosa Creek is one of the rare trout-stream jewels in southeastern New Mexico.

THE STREAM'S CLARITY astonishes and intimidates. Tumbling from pocket water to deeper holes to riffle-runs, its transparency makes it difficult to see where air ends and liquid begins. It intimidates because the trout's window is so crystalline, every detail outside their aqueous environment is undistorted. The fish have a heightened vigilance for predators when the water is this clear.

Fortunately for the angler, trout that reside in small New Mexico streams must constantly be on the prowl for food. These trout will take a buggy-looking Lime Trude dry fly if it is presented in such a way that the fish don't catch sight of the angler. Because the water is as clear as a pane of glass, you must maintain an extremely low or hidden profile.

The Pre-Cambrian granite that makes up much of the Vallecitos River bed creates a tremendous variety of runs, riffles, pockets, and deep holes. The most effective fishing technique for this water is to crouch behind in-stream boulders and drape your cast over rocks between you and the trout-holding spots. Your profile will be masked by the boulder so as not to alert the fish; and by draping line and leader over rocks you can eliminate or reduce line-drag on your fly.

The mesmerizing beauty of clear Rocky Mountain water tumbling down through dark granite slabs creates strong memories of pure enjoyment.

From US 285 just north of Ojo Caliente, turn west on NM 111 and drive through the classic northern New Mexico villages of Vallecitos and Cañon Plaza for about twenty miles. Turn west on FR 274 and drive about three miles, cross the river, and access public water.

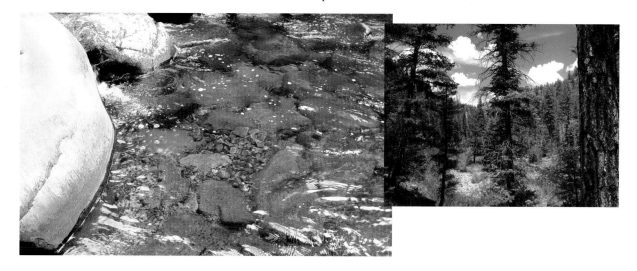

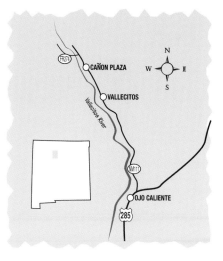

White Water Creek

THE CATWALK ATTRACTS visitors from all over the world. Tourists with cameras meander up and down the hanging metal trail, chatting and snapping photos of this unique point of interest. The canyon is so narrow you feel as if you can reach out and touch both sides with your arms spread; yet the walls are nearly one hundred feet high. It is one of the most interesting rivers in New Mexico.

Gold and silver mines were developed in this gorge in 1889. In order to provide electricity to the mill and supply water, a four-inch pipe was suspended by drilling brace holes in the solid rock walls. It carried water from three miles upstream to the mill site. Four years later more water was needed, so an 18-inch pipe was added parallel to the original. This conduit required constant maintenance and was dubbed the "Catwalk" by the workmen.

The mill operated until about 1913, and there were few visitors to the area until the late 1930s after the CCC constructed the Catwalk as a recreational attraction. In 1961 the Forest Service built the present-day metal path. It is a fascinating place.

Underneath the walkway, White Water Creek flows clear and cool in the late season. The stream is teeming with wild rainbow trout who come readily to Spent Partridge Caddis dry flies. The casting is tight. You may be able to execute the traditional overhead cast, but it also requires side-armed and cross-body casts to reach the likely spots. Your best results will come when you cover a lot of water with multiple casts.

White Water Creek offers tremendous entertainment for every member of the family. Many shaded picnic tables invite casual relaxation along the stream. The trail is an easy hike, making this extraordinary canyon available to the most casual explorer. Birds, mammals, and lizards offer a diverse array of wildlife viewing. There are even stairways down from the Catwalk to the river for access to natural swimming and wading pools.

White Water Creek flows west from the Mogollon Mountains in the Gila National Forest to the town of Glenwood. Drive west on NM 174 to the Catwalk parking and picnic area.

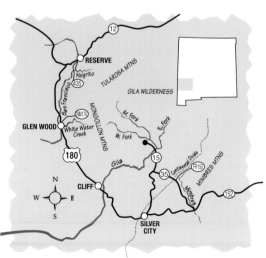

River Magnetism

ANGLERS WILL TELL you it is the fish that beckon them to the river. The trout are there waiting. They will not come to you; you need to go to them. But most of the allure is found in the river itself. Each has its own personality, its own character, its own color and sound, its own unique attraction.

Some rivers are bright and cheery and openly welcome you to explore their banks. Their cool currents turn the warmest summer day into a pleasant and comfortable outing. Other rivers are secretive and brooding, cold, and dark as they flow under the shadows of cliffs and trees. Submerged boulders lie in wait to slip you off your feet.

Some streams are hard to know, their flows in hiding or in difficult places to reach. Others are friendly and accessible and encourage your companionship.

Then there are the mysterious ones, rivers that won't let you know exactly what they are all about. On sunny days, their waters are clear and sparkling, singing a pleasant melody as they wind their way down the canyon. But when clouds roll in, muting the light into a dull gray, they are guarded and dour.

All of our rivers can be extremely generous one day and unforgiving and selfish the next. That's the nature of New Mexico streams.

We have visited rivers in the dead of winter when the cold, crisp air penetrated our layered clothing and caused goose pimples to form on our skin. We have fished in the spring when everything feels fresh and new and bright. The summer is a pleasant time to fish with the high sun warming everything. In the fall the earth's colors grow softer and muted. And as winter approaches again there is an urgency to spend just a little more time on the water before it ices over. No matter when you go to a New Mexico river it will always be interesting and you will find rewards.

To create this book we have driven countless miles to access the streams in every corner of the state. Every trip has been an adventure anew, whether we had visited a stream before or if it was new water for us. We have benefited from the joy of just being there and we hope to pass that joy on to you in these pages. We have spent hours upon hours exploring each stream. We shared the angling experience that each stream provided. We cherish every moment.

Still, within us the river magnetism persists. We can't drive by or walk near a stream without feeling the seduction of the moving water. It draws us to streamside and demands our attention. And we are thankful for this.

We encourage you to explore some of the places we have. Approach each stream with awe and appreciation for the wild beauty that surrounds our waterways and the life it brings. Spend time with each of them and share your experience with others. No two streams are alike and the same stream is different each time you visit it.

Our final wish is that all of us hold New Mexico streams precious. We are not blessed with an abundance of creeks, streams, and rivers. Each one is beautiful in its own right when you take the time to appreciate it. It is most important that we preserve their beauty. Thoughtless people have left their litter to blemish the beauty. Other writers have stated the obvious before us, but we wish to reiterate it here. Take the time to enjoy these precious places, but leave nothing behind except for your footsteps.

In mornings and evenings and all through the days, our enchanting New Mexico streams will share the beauty of the places they flow.

About the Authors

RAY SHEWNACK and BILL FRANGOS have a passion for fly-fishing New Mexico streams. Both grew up in Albuquerque and were introduced to the state's mountains and rivers at a young age.

As young adults, they independently developed an appreciation of our trout-filled streams and became proficient at fly-fishing them.

When they were serving together on the Board of Directors of New Mexico Trout, a friendship was forged. After several years and multiple fishing trips, an idea began to evolve. They waded in the rivers side by side and discussed flies and techniques. They took in the enchanting beauty. They shared personal experiences about different rivers while resting with a sandwich and snack. They explored their individual insights about New Mexico streams and the rewards they gained from them. They formulated the concept for this book.

Their common bond was a pure appreciation of the places and the desire to share the unique beauty of each stream in New Mexico with others.

Even after all the miles of driving and all the hours together, they still like fishing together.